Knights and Castles

GARETH STEVENS
GS
PUBLISHING
A Member of the WRC Media Family of Companies

by Fiona Macdonald

Consultant:
Richard Tames

This edition first published in 2005 by
Gareth Stevens Publishing
A WRC Media Company
330 West Olive Street, Suite 100
Milwaukee, Wisconsin 53212 USA

ISBN 0-8368-4997-3

This U.S. edition copyright © 2005 by Gareth Stevens, Inc.

Original edition copyright © 2004 by ticktock Entertainment Ltd.
First published in Great Britain in 2005 by ticktock Media Ltd.,
Unit 2, Orchard Business Centre, North Farm Road, Tunbridge
Wells, Kent, TN2 3XF, United Kingdom.

Gareth Stevens series editor: Dorothy L. Gibbs
Gareth Stevens art direction and cover design: Tammy West

Picture credits (t=top, b=bottom, c=center, l=left, r=right)
Alamy: 13tl, 16-17, 17tl, 22-23. Album-online: 10br. Ancient Art and
Architecture: 5tr, 7tr. Art Archive: 8c, 9l (both), 13br, 15 (all), 21cr,
21br. Bodleian Library: 1, 5cr, 5br, 11cr, 18-19, 19r (all). Bridgeman
Art Library: 5l, 11bl. British Museum: 21tr. Corbis: 2-3, 4, 6-7, 10-11 t,
12-13, 17r (both), 21l. Royal Armouries: 7br, 11 tr, 11 br. Ticktock: 8l,
8br, 9tr, 9br, 13tr, 14-15, 20t, 22tl, 23 (all).

Every effort has been made to trace the copyright holders for the
photos used in this book. The publisher apologizes, in advance, for
any unintentional omissions and would be pleased to insert appropriate
acknowledgments in any subsequent edition of this publication.

Printed in China

1 2 3 4 5 6 7 8 9 09 08 07 06 05

Contents

Medieval Knights   4

War on Horseback   6

Weapons and Armor   8

Charge!   10

Fighting for Fun   12

The First Castles   14

Walls, Moats,
and Dungeons   16

Under Attack!   18

Castle Fun   20

Ruins and Legends   22

Glossary   24

Words in the glossary
are printed in **boldface**
type the first time they
appear in the text.

Medieval Knights

Knights were brave fighting men in medieval times, which were the Middle Ages — from about AD 500 to 1500. They promised to to fight loyally for kings and **lords**. In return, they received land, treasure, and castles.

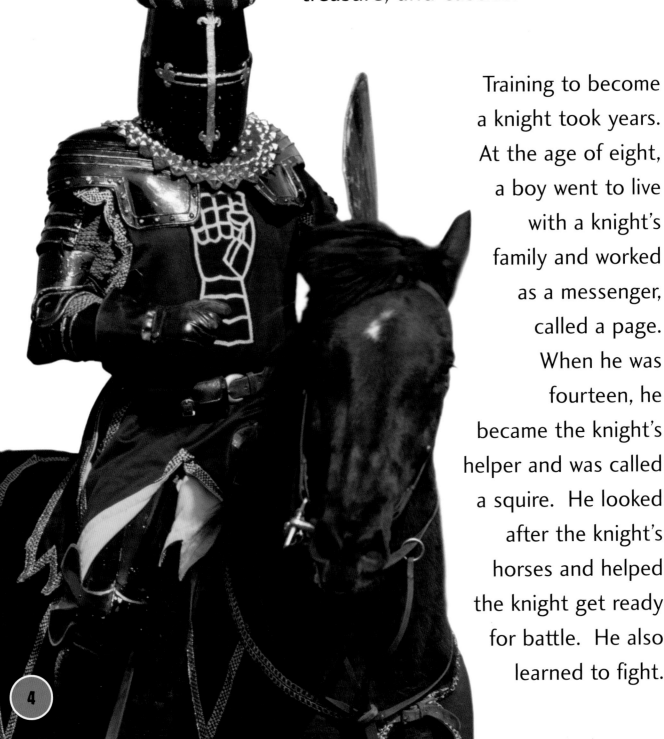

Training to become a knight took years. At the age of eight, a boy went to live with a knight's family and worked as a messenger, called a page. When he was fourteen, he became the knight's helper and was called a squire. He looked after the knight's horses and helped the knight get ready for battle. He also learned to fight.

The Life of a Knight

A knight hoped that his fame as a fighter would live on after his death.

A knight fought to protect the Christian religion.

A knight was expected to be helpful, polite, and respectful, especially to women.

At twenty-one, a squire became a knight in a special ceremony called "dubbing." The squire knelt in front of a king, a queen, or a lord, who tapped him on the shoulder with a sword and said, "Arise, Sir Knight."

War on Horseback

Knights fought on horseback, riding splendid warhorses called destriers. These horses were specially **bred** to be strong, fast, and obedient. Destriers were often very fierce, even kicking and biting their knights' enemies. **Wealthy** knights took two horses with them to a battle, in case one was killed or injured.

Good warhorses were expensive. They could cost as much as new cars cost today.

Knights used teams of packhorses to carry weapons and armor, and teams of cart horses pulled wagons loaded with **loot** won in battle.

Only the richest knights could afford armor for their horses.

A knight steered his horse using leather reins attached to a bit, which was a metal bar that was placed inside the horse's mouth.

Sharp-pointed metal spurs were attached to the heels of a knight's boots. He pressed the spurs against his horse's sides to make the horse run faster.

Weapons and Armor

To fight their enemies, knights used long swords with very sharp edges, for slashing, and short, pointed swords, for stabbing through armor. Knights also carried **daggers**.

Knights attacked enemies with **maces**, war hammers, and battle-axes, and they used wood or metal shields to help protect themselves from enemy weapons.

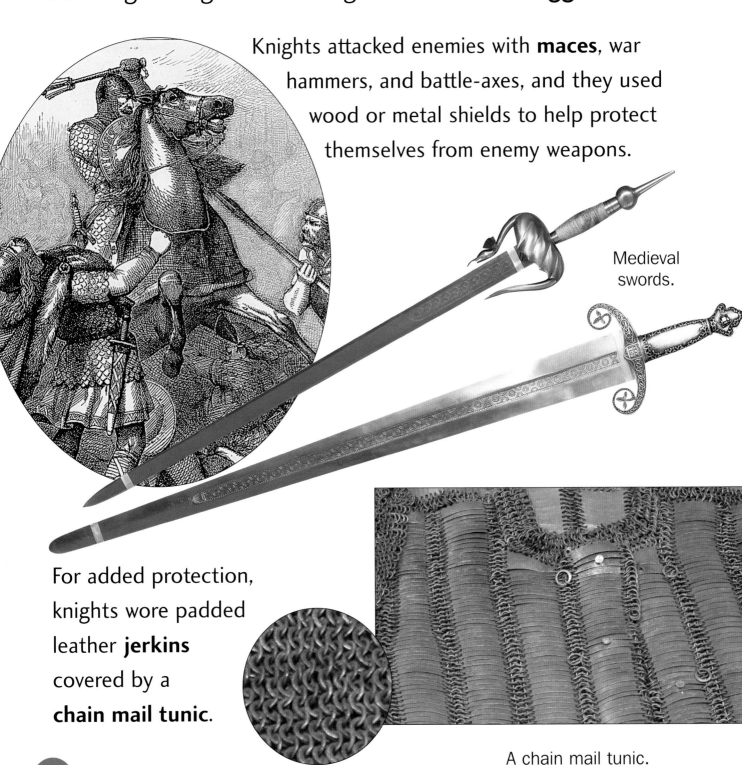

Medieval swords.

For added protection, knights wore padded leather **jerkins** covered by a **chain mail tunic**.

A chain mail tunic.

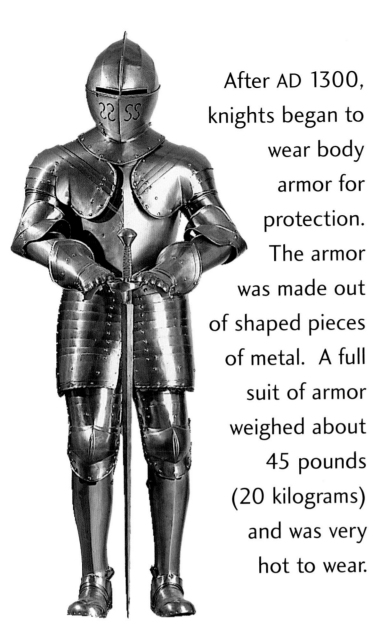

After AD 1300, knights began to wear body armor for protection. The armor was made out of shaped pieces of metal. A full suit of armor weighed about 45 pounds (20 kilograms) and was very hot to wear.

Armor from the early 1500s.

Knights displayed a family badge called a **coat of arms** on their shields or armor to help identify them.

A knight wore a protective helmet that covered his head and face. He could see out through a movable **visor**.

Metal gloves called gauntlets protected a knight's arms and hands.

Charge!

At the beginning of a battle, knights on horseback stood side by side, in rows, facing the enemy. Then, suddenly, they charged forward at top speed, shouting fierce battle cries.

A battle scene from the **Bayeux tapestry**.

Some knights carried **lances**. A lance could be used to knock an enemy off his horse. A knight on the ground was easier to attack and might also be trampled by the horses.

A battle scene from the movie *Excalibur*.

Ordinary soldiers fought on foot, using **pikes** to stab at knights on horseback. They also attacked knights with **longbows** and **crossbows**.

A skilled longbowman could shoot ten arrows a minute and hit targets more than 300 yards (275 meters) away.

Medieval Artifacts

Longbows were made of wood from **yew** trees. The arrows had sharp metal tips.

Crossbows fired metal bolts that could smash through armor.

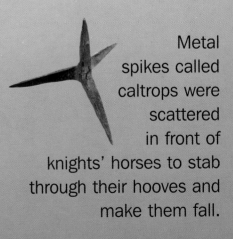

Metal spikes called caltrops were scattered in front of knights' horses to stab through their hooves and make them fall.

Fighting for Fun

In peacetime, knights fought **mock** battles using **blunt** weapons. Kings, queens, lords, and ladies all came to watch. These competitions, which were called jousts or tournaments, helped knights practice their skills.

In a joust, two knights on horseback charged toward each with wooden lances. The goal was for one of the knights to knock the other knight off his horse.

The knight who lost the joust had to give his horse and armor to the winner.

Actors perform a jousting competition.

During a mock battle, a knight wore a tunic called a surcoat over his armor. The surcoat was decorated with the knight's family coat of arms.

Knights topped their helmets with **crests** shaped like birds or monsters.

Colorful tents sheltered knights and audiences at tournaments.

13

The First Castles

In the Middle Ages, castles were the biggest and strongest buildings around. During wars, they were safe forts that protected soldiers from the enemy. Castles were also the splendid homes of rich and powerful kings and lords.

The first castles were built in about AD 900. They were wooden towers called keeps. After AD 1050, castle builders piled up earth to make steep hills, called mottes, and built wooden keeps on top of them.

A stone keep at York, in England.

A strong, wooden fence surrounded a motte. The area inside the fence was known as a bailey. Soldiers in the castle used the bailey to keep their horses safe and to store food supplies.

A motte and bailey castle from the Bayeux tapestry.

From about 800 BC to AD 200, the **Celts** built stone towers, called brochs, in Scotland.

Early castles and forts were built using simple tools and lots of muscle. There were no power tools or big machines in the Middle Ages.

Walls, Moats, and Dungeons

After AD 1000, many castles were built of stone. They had huge stone keeps, surrounded by high stone walls that were 3 feet (1 m) thick — or more!

Castle walls were made of earth and stone **rubble**, pounded together and covered, on both sides, with strong stone blocks.

Holes called machicolations for dropping rocks on enemies.

Narrow slits for shooting arrows.

Castles were surrounded by a deep, water-filled ditch called a moat. The moat could be crossed only by means of a **drawbridge**, which could be pulled up to keep enemies from entering the castle.

Castles were often used as prisons. Some had dark, damp dungeons underneath the keep floor.

The keep.

Stone walls topped with **battlements** and walkways.

Small towers made castle walls stronger. The towers were used as lookout posts.

When enemies managed to get across a castle's drawbridge, a **portcullis** was quickly dropped to keep them from entering the main castle door.

Inside castle towers, narrow, winding, stone staircases made it difficult for attackers to use their swords.

Under Attack!

Enemies tried to capture castles in many different ways. Sometimes, they dug holes under castle walls to make the walls fall down. Often, they crashed through castle gates with **battering rams**.

When attacking armies **besieged** a castle, they camped close by and blocked off all the roads. They also poisoned wells and streams and kept any fresh food from reaching people inside the castle walls.

People trapped inside a castle under attack often had only two choices — surrender, and probably be killed, or starve to death!

The people in the castle fought back, throwing stones and spears and even dropping red-hot sand onto attackers' heads.

Medieval Warfare

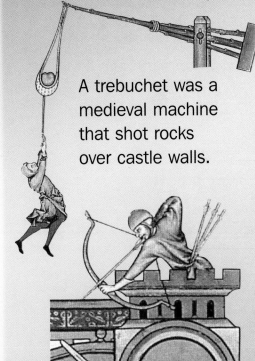

A trebuchet was a medieval machine that shot rocks over castle walls.

Longbowmen shot arrows at attackers from battlements.

When a castle was captured, the captain of the guard had to hand over the keys to the enemy.

Castle Fun

When life at a castle was peaceful, kings, lords, knights, and their families liked to have fun. They invited friends and important visitors to their castles and entertained them with feasts, music, and dancing.

Lords, knights, and **noble** ladies rode out into fields with tamed hawks. The hawks were trained to catch rabbits and small birds and bring them to their handlers.

A hawk.

Knights hunted on horseback with fierce hunting dogs. They loved to hunt deer and wild boar in the forests.

Many castles had large, parklike gardens, with fountains, statues, flowers, and fruit trees. Noble ladies, especially, liked to spend time in castle gardens.

Medieval Life

In the Middle Ages, people ate with knives, spoons, and fingers. They did not have forks.

Jesters, or fools, made people laugh at castle feasts.

Chess became popular in the early Middle Ages. This knight chess piece is more than 850 years old.

Ruins and Legends

Beginning in about 1400, castles came under attack by new weapons called cannons. These big iron tubes were filled with gunpowder and fired huge stone balls that had the power to smash down castle walls.

In 1460, at Roxburgh Castle, King James II of Scotland was killed when his own new cannon exploded. He was showing his wife how it worked.

By the end of the Middle Ages, kings, lords, and knights wanted stylish, more comfortable houses, and many castles fell into **ruin**.

Every year, millions of today's tourists visit the castle ruins found across Europe.

Since the end of the Middle Ages, many legends have sprung up about castles. Some people believe they have seen ghosts in spooky castle passageways.

Many fairy tales have been inspired by ruined castles like this one in France.

Performers **reenacting** a battle between medieval knights.

Glossary

battering rams: huge, heavy wooden beams or tree trunks

battlements: walled platforms with spaces through which to fire weapons

Bayeux tapestry: a 230-foot- (70-m-) long wall hanging, with embroidered scenes of the Norman (French) conquest of England in 1066

besieged: surrounded for an attack

blunt: not sharp

bred: produced as offspring through planned mating

Celts: the main culture of people in Europe from about 800 BC to AD 200

chain mail: a type of armor made up of thousands of small metal rings that are linked as if woven together

coat of arms: special designs, badges, or emblems used from about AD 1200 to identify different families and their positions and importance in society

crests: showy or decorative figures

crossbows: short bows that shoot short arrows by pulling a trigger

daggers: short, doubled-edged knives

drawbridge: a huge, heavy door that was raised and lowered over a moat to stop or allow entry into a castle

jerkins: sleeveless, collarless jackets

lances: long, heavy spears

longbows: bows that shoot arrows by pulling back their bowstrings by hand

loot: valuable goods taken in a war

lords: men of high rank who, in the Middle Ages, were powerful landowners

maces: heavy clubs with a spiked metal ball at one end

mock: pretend or acted out

noble: having a high rank in society

pikes: sharp spikes on long poles

portcullis: an iron gate that could be lowered to protect a castle doorway

reenacting: repeating the actions of earlier events

rubble: small stones or pieces of brick

ruin: damage or disrepair

tunic: a long shirt that looks like a sleeveless dress

visor: the hinged front piece of a helmet that moves up and down over the face

wealthy: having a lot of money and valuable possessions

yew: an evergreen tree or shrub that has heavy, fine-grained wood